On the Move

CARS

Ursula Pang

PowerKiDS press

PK Beginners

Look at all the cars!

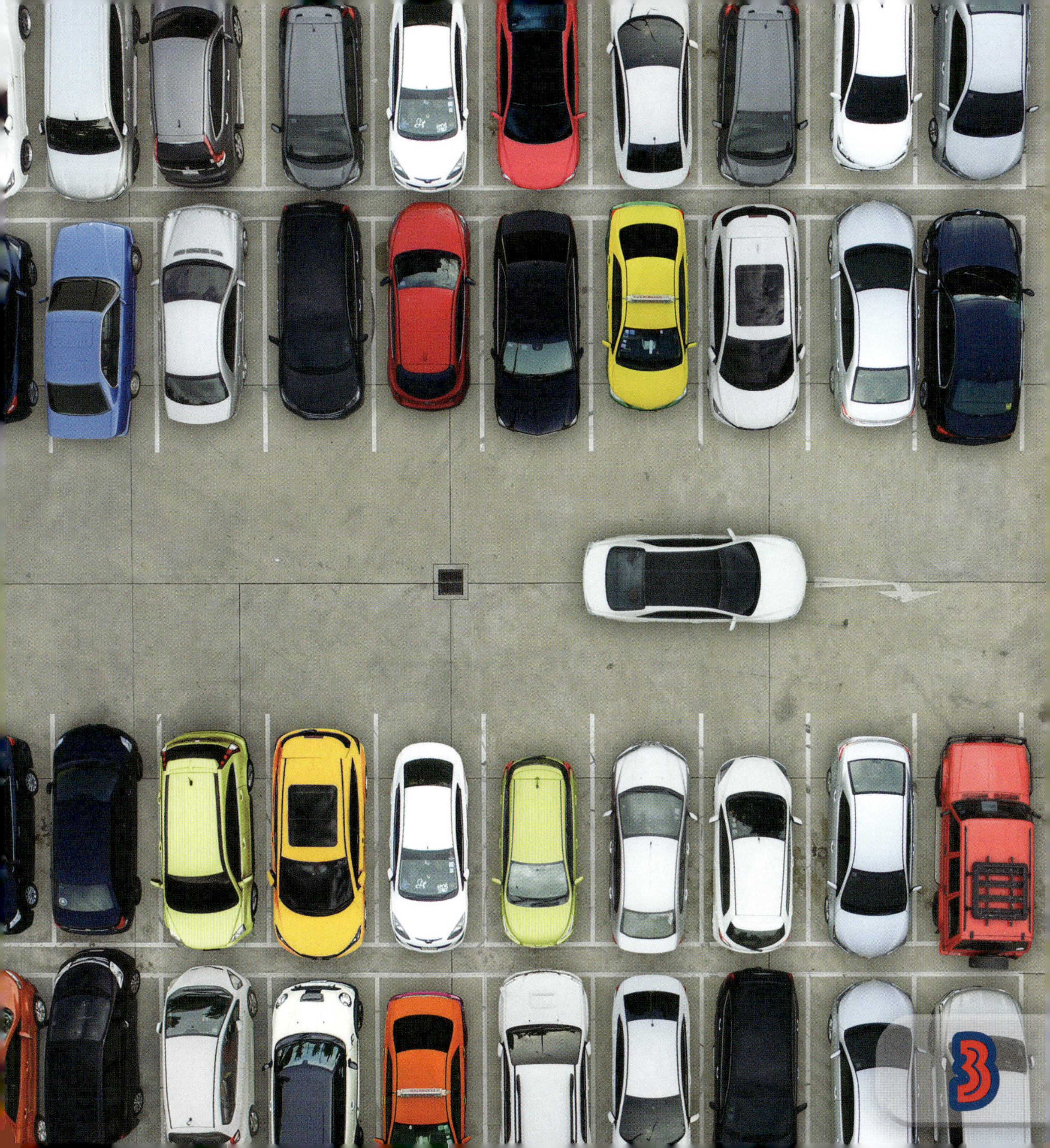

People use cars
to get around.

Cars need a driver.

DRIVER

Do not bother
the driver.
That is not safe.

Seatbelts keep us safe in the car.

SEATBELT

Always be careful
around car traffic.

Cars can be big
or small.

Some cars carry a lot of people!

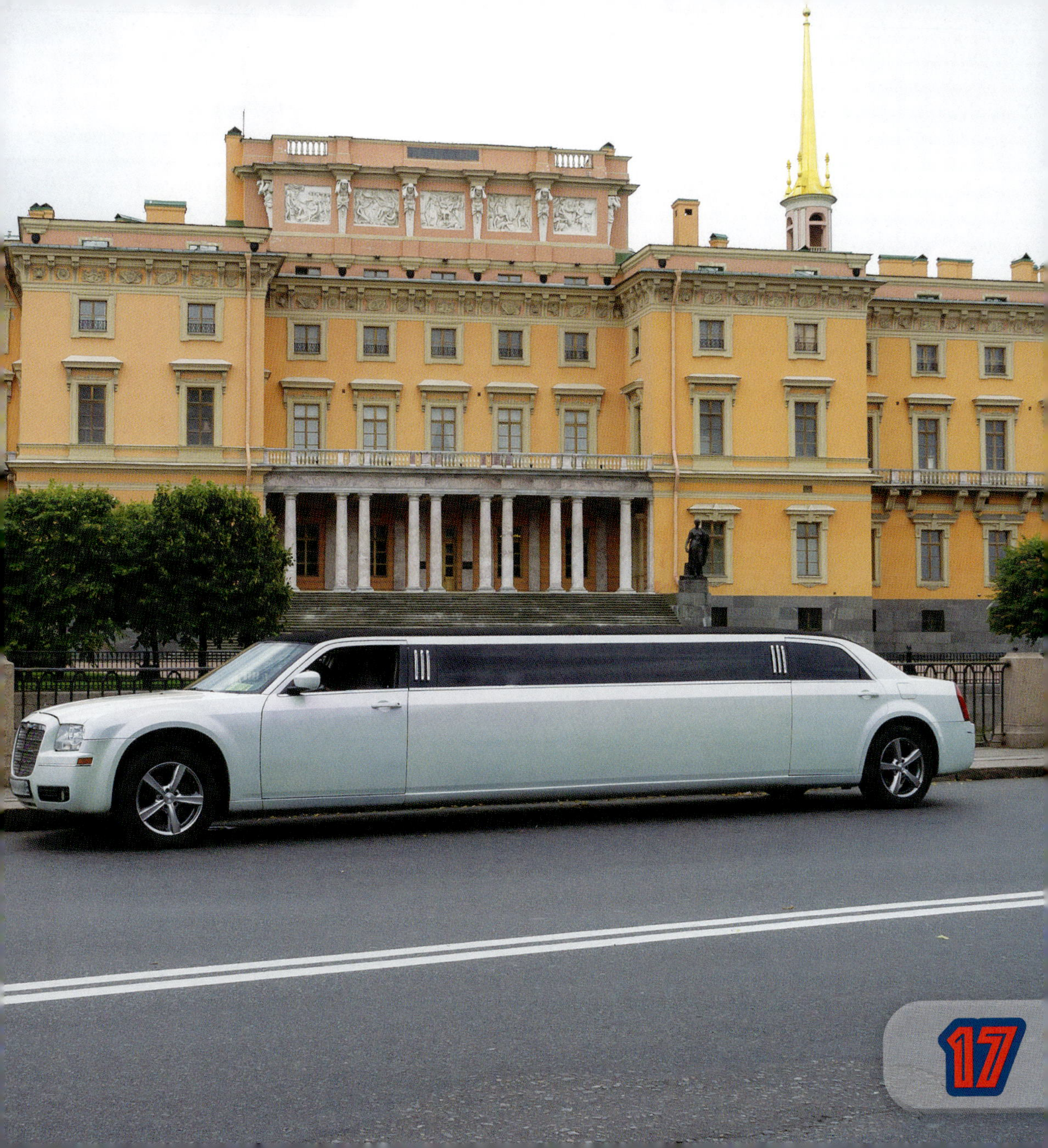

Some people
race cars.
They go fast!

1

Some people like long car trips.

Have you ever been on a long car trip?

Published in 2025 by The Rosen Publishing Group, Inc.
2544 Clinton Street, Buffalo, NY 14224

First Edition

Editor: Greg Roza
Book Design: Rachel Rising

Photo Credits: Cover, p.1 Camerasandcoffee/Shutterstock.com; p. 3 non c/Shutterstock.com; p. 5 Anton_AV/Shutterstock.com; p. 7 michaeljung/Shutterstock.com; p. 9 Prostock-studio/Shutterstock.com; p. 11 Sergii Kozii/Shutterstock.com; p. 13 e2dan/Shutterstock.com; p. 15 Maria Avvakumova/Shutterstock.com; p. 17 Khalangot Sergey L/Shutterstock.com; p. 19 tcharts/Shutterstock.com; p. 21 Juice Dash/Shutterstock.com; p. 23 Nickolya/Shutterstock.com.

Library of Congress Cataloging-in-Publication Data

Names: Pang, Ursula, author.
Title: Cars / Ursula Pang.
Description: Buffalo : PowerKids Press, (2024) | Series: On the move
Identifiers: LCCN 2023051230 (print) | LCCN 2023051231 (ebook) | ISBN 9781499444636 (library binding) | ISBN 9781499444629 (paperback) | ISBN 9781499444643 (ebook)
Subjects: LCSH: Automobiles--Juvenile literature.
Classification: LCC TL147 .P36 2024 (print) | LCC TL147 (ebook) | DDC 629.222--dc23/eng/20231107
LC record available at https://lccn.loc.gov/2023051230
LC ebook record available at https://lccn.loc.gov/2023051231

Manufactured in the United States of America

CPSIA Compliance Information: Batch #CSPK25. For further information contact Rosen Publishing at 1-800-237-9932.